Challenging Change

Challenging Change

*Five Steps for Dealing
Positively With Change*

Holly DeForest
Mary Steinberg

SkillPath Publications
Mission, KS

Project Editor: Kelly Scanlon

Editor: Jane Doyle Guthrie

Page Layout: Premila Malik Borchardt and Rod Hankins

Cover Design: Rod Hankins and David Kuhn

ISBN: 1-57294-049-2

Library of Congress Card Catalog Number: 96-67063

10 9 8 7 6 5   06 07 08 09 10

Printed in the United States of America

Contents

Introduction

Judith sat in her car waiting for the light to change and reflected on all that had happened at work that day. Tom, a mid-level manager in the Human Resources Department, had been told his job was being abolished due to an impending reorganization. Judith thought: "I knew it was a possibility, but I can't believe it. He's been with this company eighteen years—same as me. What if I'm next?" She knew she should have talked to him but didn't even know how to begin. "And what can I say to my employees? They're worried too. I heard one of them say he knows that management just can't be trusted because we're withholding information. Until I know everything, how can I say anything?" When Judith finally turned into her driveway, she was surprised and happy to see her daughter Molly's car. "It will be good to talk to her. I just hope she hasn't brought weird Randy with her." Molly met her mom at the door and said: "I can't wait to tell you. Randy and I are getting married!" Judith leaned against the wall and said out loud, "Do I have any control over my life anymore?"

This book is for anyone who has had circumstances turn out differently from what was originally expected and who has experienced the feeling of loss of control. It doesn't matter if the difference was positive or negative—the question is, were there unexpected changes? Most of you are probably saying,

"Sure, during last year. And last month, and last week, and even yesterday. In fact, not only were things different than expected, I'm not sure I remember how they were supposed to go." The primary reason for a reaction like this could be the pace and magnitude of change you face in today's world.

How are you reacting to change? Lewis Carroll wrote in *Through the Looking Glass*, "It takes all the running you can do to keep in the same place." Running in place has probably never been a good idea, but in today's world where terms such as "riding on the information super highway," "surfing the Internet," and "navigating the whitewater rapids of change" have become part of everyday speech, running in place is going to get you flattened (or worse)!

How Fast Is Change?

In their book *A Survival Guide to the Stress of Organizational Change*, Price Pritchett and Ron Pound say there was more information produced between the thirty-year period of 1965 to 1995 than in the five thousand-year period of 3000 B.C. to 1965.

To illustrate how fast the rate of change has been accelerating, think about how advancing technology and global communication have intensified the need to stay current. For example, think about the impact of Johannes Gutenberg's work with the printing press versus the impact of the computer on their respective times.

Contrary to popular belief, Gutenberg neither invented movable type (the Chinese did) nor did he print the first book. What he did was invent movable type for the Western world and make printing practical. Amazingly, his method of using type remained essentially unchanged for almost *five centuries*. His use of movable type and the resulting capabilities and products rendered one of the greatest changes in history, but it was probably years (centuries) before the majority of the world's population was *directly* affected.

Compare that to the advance of computers. In 1953, there were only about one hundred computers in use in the entire world. It is probably unnecessary to say any more for you to understand the differences in the pace and impact of change between the introduction of the computer and the introduction of movable type. Unlike the ability to remain illiterate during Gutenberg's time, is it possible for you to remain computer illiterate during these times?

Are you able to stay current with all that's happening that has an impact on you? On your employees or others associated with you? On your organization? Even if you're comfortable with and knowledgeable about computers, are there other changes that affect you that you're not so comfortable with or knowledgeable about? What about changes in technology, economic indicators, social issues, political agendas, or domestic and foreign markets and their potential impact?

So What Can You Do?

You react to these and other changes, as do your fellow employees and your organization. If your reaction is simply one of running in place—or even worse, losing ground—the implications can be devastating. You must be proactive. As a change leader, it is your job to help yourself, those you work with, and your organization deal with everyday needs, meet quality and production requirements, keep up with competition, seize opportunities, etc., etc., etc. And you must do this in a constantly shifting environment.

Books and articles talk about managing change, living with change, and surviving change. Sounds pretty passive. Isn't it time to *challenge* change? That is, confront it boldly?

Challenge? Isn't That a Little Harsh?

One meaning of "challenge" implies calling to a halt—not what's meant in this book. You can't order most change to halt! But another definition offers the idea of a dare, or an invitation to compete. Think back on positive competitions you have engaged in, such as participating in a novel academic or athletic event, learning a new skill, or overcoming an unexpected adversity. In other words, *challenging* change. Remember how it was at the end—you felt great, or smarter, or proud of yourself. This is how you can feel if you learn to challenge change. Be bold; "issue an invitation" to change and meet it head on.

The five-step "Challenging Change" model presented in Chapter 1 and described in Chapters 2 through 6 offers a rational, "doable" approach that will enable you to prepare for, face, explore options for, take charge of, and monitor change. The exercises included throughout these chapters are designed to get you involved immediately through a series of actions relevant to real changes you face. As Winston Churchill urged, "Difficulties mastered are opportunities won."

Chapter One

Issue the Invitation

"If a man will begin with certainties, he shall end in doubts; but, if he will be content to begin with doubts, he shall end in certainties."
—Francis Bacon

When people issue invitations to others, they often add a note to "R.S.V.P." so they can know how many (if any) people are going to come. In looking at a challenge to change as an invitation, you won't need to add that R.S.V.P.—change *is going to show up.*

5

Change Is Constant

Although it sounds like a clash in terms to say so, constant change has become our status quo. Actually what's interesting is that this isn't new. Benjamin Disraeli, the famous British politician and writer, said in a speech that "Change is inevitable in a progressive society. Change is constant." If he called change "constant" in 1867, what would he call it now?

Tom calls it overwhelming. (Tom's the mid-level manager discussed in the Introduction.) He recently transferred to the Midwest as a result of the reorganization in his company. His wife Ellen did not join him for two months, as she had difficulty finding employment in the new city. Now, nine months after his transfer, another restructuring is afoot, and Tom's job is being abolished—which means he'll probably have to relocate again if he wants to stay with the company. Tom isn't sure what positions are available or in which offices openings exist. He has spent so much time traveling on his job he really doesn't know people at this office that well. He certainly hasn't had time to meet people outside of work. He feels out of the information loop, both professionally and personally. As for his family, Tom's two teenagers have told him they really like their new school and are happy they made this move. Ellen just received a promotion to a managerial position and is already involved in local community activities.

Tom called a friend in the city where he used to live and told him he knew he faced more changes in the past nine months than his grandparents did in their lifetimes. What really scared him was that he had felt so secure with this company for so long—eighteen years. And it seemed like it all changed overnight. He went on to say that he wondered if he still knew how to interview, because it had been so long since he had to go through one. Things were happening so fast that Tom almost felt paralyzed.

If changes on your horizons (or under your feet) are happening fast, how are you reacting? Exercise 1 asks you to think about what's going on in your life, but not to think about your answers too long. Most people have so much information coming at them from so many directions that they end up reacting rather than taking the time to sort things out. That's what this exercise asks you to do—just react. Here you'll create a base line against which to measure your approach to the subsequent exercises in the book.

Exercise

What's Happening to You?

The purpose of this exercise is to start you thinking (but only a bit) about what may be influencing your approach to change. All you need to do is react to the following questions *quickly*. These questions aren't in any particular order, don't necessarily have anything to do with one another, and cover a myriad of subjects. Some are important to your ability to challenge change, and some may not be. If there doesn't seem to be any logic to one or more, think of them as a reflection of how life can be at times. There's no need to provide a written response.

1. What do you do to relax? Do you relax?

2. What recent risk have you taken and what did you learn from this experience?

3. How do you measure customer needs? Customer satisfaction?

4. If you own a business, what is your vision for it? How do you know if you are headed toward it?

5. What kind of person were you when you chose your current career? Have you changed? What prompted those changes?

6. How do you scan for information you need?

7. If you are a manager, what managerial skills do you have?

8. How do you keep up-to-date on government policies or regulations that may affect your business?

9. If you have employees, how do you think they view you? Do they look to you for direction? Do you want them to?

10. If you have children, how do you think they view you? Do they look to you for direction? Do you want them to?

11. How do you keep motivated?

12. What do you believe are some of the old ways of doing business that can't lead businesses into the future?

13. How do you acknowledge the contributions of others? At work? At home?

14. How do you articulate your goals and expectations?

15. Do you know how to give constructive feedback? Do you know how to receive it?

16. In times of change, do you consider what has remained stable in your life and how that can help?

17. What techniques have you developed for dealing with change?

18. What techniques for dealing with change do you see in others you work with? Or live with?

19. Are you willing to try new ideas and approaches to issues?

20. Two years ago, you never would have thought you would do what?

21. If you have young children, do you yell at them to "stop yelling"?

22. How do you reward yourself?

23. Do you use the latest technology to its fullest potential for your needs in your business life? In your personal life?

24. What two things went really well for you recently? What was your role in each?

25. What two things didn't go so well? What was your role?

26. If you have teenagers, have you ever said, "You call that music?" If so, do you know what music you were talking about?

27. When several things are going on at the same time, how do you decide which changes to pay attention to?

28. Do you ever say, "I never would have thought of that"?

29. What are your hot buttons? What or who has pushed them lately?

30. Can you admit when you just don't know?

31. How many times have you moved?

32. Can you play Nintendo? Do you know what Nintendo is?

33. How many career changes have you made?

34. How many changes have you had in significant relationships?

35. What new skill(s) have you learned this year? What have you taught someone else this year?

36. Can you listen in a nonjudgmental way?

37. Do you ever talk to others about how they handle change?

Believe it or not, your daily life is affected by most of these questions. If you're like most people, though, you haven't paid attention to what affects your behavior, or what your strengths are, or where your weaknesses lie. The next time you see some of these questions in this book, you'll be asked to approach them in a different manner—one that will assist you in challenging change.

Reactions to Change

To *challenge* change makes sense when you consider the tough decisions businesses face as a result of fierce competition, increasing/decreasing government regulations, rapid technological changes, and disparate workforce skills. The effects of these and other changes on organizations is reflected in how businesses are downsizing, rightsizing, dividing, merging, growing, collapsing, and just about *anything* but staying the same.

In addition to organizations, people too are reacting—as reflected in more frequent absenteeism, greater use of employee assistance programs, increased number of mid-life (and young-life and older-life) crises, enhanced feelings of helplessness, and in the extreme, increased workplace violence. With these harsh realities of current life, a bold approach to meeting change head-on seems imperative. One way to do this is to *challenge* change, which for most people probably means adapting to a new model of reacting.

The five-step "Challenging Change" model on the next page offers a graduated approach to help you deal positively with change.

Challenging Change Model

Step 1: **Prepare for change.** Examine your readiness to challenge change with emphasis on required leadership competencies.

Step 2: **Face the change.** Highlight a specific change to work on and begin to gather information about the change and your reactions to it.

Step 3: **Explore options for change.** Share the information you've gathered with others and provide opportunities for it to be confirmed or refuted.

Step 4: **Take charge of change.** Identify specific actions required to implement the change with the support of those affected.

Step 5: **Monitor change.** Measure progress, determine ways for continuous learning, and celebrate.

The ultimate goal of this model is to enable you to *challenge* change rather than ignore it or feel overwhelmed by it. The less overwhelmed you are by change, the better. Not only is change constant, it is rarely predictable. Benjamin Disraeli had something to say about that also: "What we anticipate seldom occurs, what we least expect generally happens." So for those days when you say "Do I have any control over my life anymore?" this model helps you take the steps needed to gain control. The next exercise will get you started.

Exercise

Slow Down Now

You were asked in Exercise 1 to consider several questions without putting much thought into them. In our ever-changing environment, this is often how decisions are made—generally not such a good idea. This exercise presents you with three of the questions from Exercise 1, along with a new question. This time, slow down and put some thought into your answers. If you truly can't answer one, consider why. Begin to pay attention to your reactions as you complete this and the other exercises that follow.

1. What two things went really well for you recently? What was your role in each?

_____

_____

_____

_____

_____

_____

_____

2. What techniques have you developed for dealing with change?

_____

_____

_____

_____

_____

_____

3. When a lot is going on at the same time, how do you decide which changes to pay attention to?

_____

_____

_____

_____

_____

4. Do you intend to complete this exercise? If not, why not?

_____

_____

_____

_____

Start to Take Time and Pay Attention

The exercise you just completed asked you to consider the roles you play and the techniques you use in dealing with change; that is, to identify those skills you use in handling many of the changes you face. Chances are you may not even be thinking about those skills when you use them.

Have you ever heard the term *unconscious competence?* It means doing something well without thinking about what it takes to do it, such as driving. In times of change, it's important to begin to pay attention to your competencies, especially those that will serve you well in *challenging* change.

The introductory paragraph to Exercise 2 directed you to begin paying attention to your reactions as you complete the exercises in this book. Question 4 was posed so you would begin to explore any resistance you may be feeling. Resistance, along with other types of reactions, plays a major role in your response to change. (Reactions to change will be explored in detail in Chapter 3.)

Marvin Weisbord, coauthor of *Discovering Common Ground,* once said, "Your own warm body is your best intervention." So take time and pay attention to what's going on with yourself. Taking time helps prepare you for the challenge. In this chapter, you have issued the invitation to change—that's important because it shows a willingness to live with some uncertainty. The next chapter introduces you to the first step from the Challenging Change model: preparing for change.

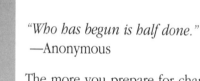

Chapter Two

Prepare for Change

"*Who has begun is half done.*"
—Anonymous

The more you prepare for change, the smoother the ride will be. In order to know what's needed to avoid the rough spots, you'll need to take a good look at yourself. Along with fastening your emotional seat belt, you may want to make some minor, or even major, adjustments. Before deciding how you'll prepare, take a second look at Judith, whose run-in with change opened this book.

One major upheaval in Judith's life involved the reorganization at her company and its potential implications for her. There are two facts we know about her: She avoided talking to someone whose job had been abolished (in spite of wondering whether it was going to happen to her), and she chose not to talk to her employees about the reorganization because she felt she didn't know all the facts. Both issues involve communication (in Judith's case, lack of) during times of change.

Do you react this way when faced with an uncomfortable change? If so, you're likely to have a bumpy ride through life.

What About Others?

Most changes that affect you will also have an effect on others. And in most cases, they too will need to prepare. As a change leader, people will be looking to you—for information, for guidance, and for reactions. And although others will turn to you, they ultimately of course must be responsible for themselves—and that sense of responsibility is the most important thing you can instill in them. In order to do that, however, you need to ready yourself first.

Al Stasa, a consultant who works with groups on issues involving change, uses the following example to illustrate the need to ready yourself before assisting others in managing change: He reminds his listeners of the instructions they receive about the use of oxygen masks if the cabin should lose pressure—the attendants say to get *yourself* ready before trying to assist anyone else.

You have to be clear on where you're going with respect to change before you can help others. Exercise 3 asks you to consider some of the behaviors that are important in discovering where you are heading.

Exercise

3

Are You Prepared?

This exercise will help increase your awareness of behaviors that are significant in times of change. Some of the statements come from the questions in Exercise 1.

Circle the letter that best describes your answer:

    a = It's my normal way of operating.

    b = I've acted this way at least once in the past year.

    c = I never act this way.

1. I am willing to try new ideas and approaches to issues.

    a ————— b ————— c

2. I talk to others about how they handle change.

    a ————— b ————— c

3. I admit when I don't know something.

    a ————— b ————— c

4. I use active listening skills.

    a ————— b ————— c

5. I strive for continual improvements.

a ——————— b ——————— c

6. I learn new skills.

a ——————— b ——————— c

Scoring key:

For each "a," give yourself 5 points.

For each "b," give yourself 3 points.

For each "c," give yourself 0 points.

Total score:

24–30	Congratulations! You understand that change is part of life and have prepared yourself to face it. You have a smooth ride ahead. You also understand the need to establish a periodic maintenance schedule.
18–23	You have a steady grip on the steering wheel as you ride through change. But you need to get a minor tune-up and establish a maintenance schedule.
13–17	You exhibit some of the important behaviors needed to prepare for change, yet your ride is probably bumpy enough to require a new set of shocks.

Below 13   It would probably be best if you asked for some assistance in preparing for change. You might want to consider the assistance of an external or internal consultant who has experience in this area. You were honest in your responses, which shows you're at least willing to fasten your seat belt!

The more you're willing to look at yourself, the better you'll see whether you're ready to face the challenges and opportunities of change. Your honest responses can lead you to an important discovery—the changes you may have to make in your own personal behavior. After all, does it make sense to assume you can remain productive in a changing environment without changing yourself?

What Else is Needed?

Several components are involved in the ability to challenge change. One important one is how prepared you are, which you explored in Exercise 3, and another is your mastery of the competencies associated with change leaders. Although much has been written about such competencies, the ones chosen for the next exercise are those that can best assist in smoothing your ride on the road of change. If you're aware of additional competencies that are important for you, add them.

Exercise

4

Change Competencies

Following is a list of six competencies and the skills associated with them. First, place a check mark (✓) by the skills you think represent your strengths. Then place an "X" next to the skills you need to improve. If a statement is not applicable to your situation, write N/A by it.

Communication

_____ I make communication a high priority.

_____ I share information with others.

_____ I ask for more information if I don't understand.

_____ I actively listen to what people have to say to me.

_____ I don't "kill the messenger."

_____ I state clearly what I expect and want.

_____ I give and solicit constructive feedback.

Problem Solving

_____ I establish both realistic short-term and long-term goals.

_____ I establish roles and responsibilities.

_____ I anticipate potential problems and opportunities related to these goals, roles, or responsibilities.

_____ I am able to filter through data to determine the root cause of problems.

_____ I use tools and techniques such as brainstorming, flowcharting, data collection, and so forth to effectively solve problems.

_____ I establish monitoring procedures to ensure problems stay solved.

_____ I involve others in all of the above.

Motivation

_____ I exhibit the behaviors I expect others to exhibit.

_____ I share authority and let people know the responsibility and accountability that go with this shared authority.

_____ I let people know the rewards and consequences that go with my expectations.

_____ I establish rewards and consequences that reflect my expectations (for example, if I expect teamwork, rewards are based on teamwork).

_____ I share credit for a job well done.

Innovation

_____ I keep current on new trends affecting my organizational and personal needs.

_____ I ask, "Are there other ways of looking at this?"

_____ I determine training needs when new technologies are introduced.

_____ I take risks.

_____ I am willing to let others take risks.

_____ I consider the outcomes of the risks I consider
taking.

Focus on Customers

_____ I know what my customers expect of me.

_____ I have systems in place to receive information about
whether my customers are satisfied with what they
receive from me.

_____ I use information from my customers to improve
the quality of the product (service) they receive.

Continuous Learning

_____ I pursue educational opportunities.

_____ I teach others.

_____ I learn from others.

_____ I learn from my mistakes.

_____ I identify and keep up to date on trends that affect
my organization or my personal life.

_____ I am involved in outside organizations in my field
of expertise.

_____ I subscribe to publications covering a wide range of
issues.

Now look back on how you marked the skills associated with the six competencies. Identify below which competency(ies) you are strongest in and which you need to develop:

Strongest _____

_____

_____

Need to Develop _____

_____

_____

Next, it's time to take a risk. If you placed a check mark by this skill under "Innovation," this should come naturally; if you didn't, please accept the following feedback. If you refuse to take risks in today's world, there'll probably be many times when you wonder whether you have any control over your life. The risk to take for this exercise is this: Share the preceding list of competencies and skills with a colleague who has knowledge of how you operate and ask him or her to identify your strengths and the areas in which you need development. Compare the two lists and discuss the similarities and differences.

Now What?

The hardest part in preparing for any endeavor is often the first step—in this case, taking an honest look at yourself as a change leader.

The good news is that once you've identified your strengths and areas for development, the strategies are often straightforward. One way to establish strategies to strengthen your skills is to simply do what the skills statements in Exercise 4 indicate. For instance, under "Problem Solving," establish realistic short-term and long-term goals if you haven't already done so. Following is a list of additional strategies for each of the six competencies you just explored (and you can probably add many others from your own experiences):

Communication

- Conduct meetings to provide information to your work group.

- Keep others informed of changes even when you don't know all the answers.

- Ask others how they want to receive information.

Problem Solving

- Attend quality improvement training.

- Incorporate problem-solving tools in your daily work.

Motivation

- Have the group identify a common goal.

- Have the group identify the roles and responsibilities of group members.

Innovation

- Do something out of the ordinary.

- Find a different use for something you have used in only one way.

Focus on Customers

- Meet with customers to determine what's important to them and how well you're doing.

- Develop a customer service questionnaire.

- Ask your work-group members to articulate who the customers are. Check to see if everyone agrees.

- Set up a reward system to acknowledge quality customer service.

- Develop training materials for customer service.

Continuous Learning

- Analyze a recent problem you've encountered in terms of how your own actions may have contributed to it.

- Teach something somewhere (this can be as simple as a two-hour presentation at a local school).

Congratulations on taking a significant first step—preparing for change. What you've accomplished involved some real work. The additional benefit is that now you can involve others. The next chapter takes you to the second step of the Challenging Change model: facing the change.

Chapter Three

Face the Change

"Would you tell me, please, which way I ought to go from here?" asked Alice.

"That depends a good deal on where you want to go to," said the Cheshire Cat.

—from *Alice's Adventure in Wonderland* by Lewis Carroll

The previous chapter revealed that you have to be clear about where you're going with respect to change. You need to know this before you can help yourself or others face change. To determine where you're going, it's essential to name the change(s) you're facing and identify the accompanying reactions. Let's plunge straight away into an exercise to help you do that, not only for yourself but also for others affected by the same change(s).

Exercise

What Are You Facing?

Each portion of the information requested below is important to complete. You will refer to your answers in this exercise throughout the remainder of the book.

1. What changes are you encountering now? Your list should include changes you have chosen, changes imposed on you, changes you look forward to, changes you have some anxiety about, and so on. In other words, try to note all the changes in your life at this time or coming up in the near future.

_____

_____

_____

_____

_____

2. Which change that you listed in question 1 most requires your attention in the near future and presents a challenge to you?

_____

_____

_____

3. What is going well with the change you identified in
question 2?

_____

_____

_____

_____

_____

_____

4. What do you need to be doing differently?

_____

_____

_____

_____

5. How are you reacting to this change?

_____

_____

_____

_____

6. How are others who will be affected reacting to this change?

_____

_____

_____

_____

_____

7. Which competencies from Exercise 4 in Chapter 2 would prove most effective in helping you face this change and deal with the reactions you identified in questions 5 and 6 of this exercise?

_____

_____

_____

_____

_____

In Exercise 2, question 3 asked, "When a lot is going on at the same time, how do you decide which changes to pay attention to?" Review your answer. Is this the method you used to choose the change you identified in question 2 of this exercise? If so, is this a reasonable method of choosing? If it's not the method you used, why not?

Why These Questions?

The questions in Exercise 5 relate to one of three categories:

- The change event itself (questions 1 through 4)

- Reactions to the change event (questions 5 and 6)

- Techniques for dealing with both the change and the reactions to it (question 7)

There's a reason for separating questions about change from questions about reactions to change. Both elements need to be addressed and, if possible, anticipated. In *Managing Transitions*, William Bridges emphasizes the importance of planning for the change event as well as the associated transition. He defines change as an external action or event that is scheduled to happen. He notes that with every change comes a transition, which he defines as the internal, psychological aspects of dealing with the change. In other words, *reactions* to change.

Dr. Bridges asserts that individuals and organizations must pay attention to both the change and the transition, indicating that if either aspect is poorly managed, problems will arise. Take a look at Tom and Judith again:

If Tom completed Exercise 5, he would include the abolishment of his position in question 2. He would probably respond in question 4 that he needs more information from his employer. Question 5 would no doubt include comments about fear over his loss of security, feelings of isolation from not knowing many people in the new city, uneasiness with how his wife and children will respond, and a sense of "paralysis."

Because Judith is trying to avoid her work issues as much as possible, she would probably list her daughter's impending marriage in question 2. Very likely her answer to question 5 would include reactions of anxiety and maybe sadness.

Both Judith and Tom feel confused and alienated, yet neither one takes control of the situation at this time. Both have stated the same dilemma in different ways—"I no longer have control over my life."

One way these two individuals could gain some control is to use selected skills associated with the competencies presented in Chapter 2. Tom would benefit by concentrating on communication and continuous learning, both at work and with his family. He wishes his employer would communicate more about what's going on. Tom should communicate with his family about what's going on. It would also benefit him to brush up on effective interviewing techniques. As for Judith, she would most likely benefit from active listening skills when she speaks to her daughter about the impending wedding plans.

The ability to determine what they can and cannot control is crucial in how Tom and Judith face change. They may not be able to control the actual event (Tom is not at a level in his organization where he establishes policy, and Judith is dealing with someone in love), but they *can* deal with and control their actions.

Take a look again at your answer to question 7 in Exercise 5. Which competencies and skills did you choose? Are there any others that could help you address the issues you raised in question 4 or your reactions to the change you identified in questions 5 and 6? Speaking of reactions, see if the following unfolds as a familiar path with regard to any change(s) in your life.

Levels of Reaction to Change

Many reactions to change are possible. But for the purposes of this discussion, they can be classified into three levels: *denial, resistance,* and *commitment.* It's important to understand where you and others are and where everyone needs to be. As a change leader, it's up to you to move yourself and influence others to move up to the level of commitment.

Levels of Reaction to Change

Level One: Denial

- Focus on past
- Wish for failure

Level Two: Resistance

- Acknowledge the change
- Focus on effects of change
- Feelings of sadness, anger, anxiety

Level Three: Commitment

- Renewed interest and increased productivity
- Future vision
- Common goals

At the *denial* level, concentration focuses on how things were done in the past. The people affected hope that the change will fail and often deny that it will really occur. They'll equate the current change with a past one that was never implemented and hope (or often, really believe) this will be the case now. In other words, if they keep busy with other things or keep their heads low, this too will pass. At this level, those involved want to keep things the way they were.

At the *resistance* level, people begin to at least acknowledge that life will be different. They begin to focus on themselves and how they will be affected. Resistance often produces a nagging sense of sadness, but those affected can't determine why. They may become angry, withdrawn, and anxious. Tempers tend to flare more than usual. People tend to resist what they perceive as a threat to the proven way of doing business. They spend more emotional energy holding on to old habits and beliefs than they would if they adopted the change.

Here are some of the common reasons why people resist change:

- A desire not to give up something they value

- A misunderstanding of the change and its ramifications

- Fear of the unknown

- Fear of failure

The good news is that energy exists at the resistance level. This state is flexible—some people just need to say "no" before saying "yes." Although decreasing resistance is crucial to the success of the change process, keep in mind that resistance is normal.

When people undergoing change reach the *commitment* level, they see (and feel) renewed interest, restored productivity, and a vision for the future. This is the level to aspire toward. When commitment occurs, people are working together for a common goal.

Unfortunately, no consistent movement or predictable time frame occurs between levels. Your (or your group's) position on the continuum depends on your ability to deal with change, how turbulent the changes are, and your skill in assisting yourself and others through the levels.

How Can You Assist?

As a change leader, it's obviously important for you to know which level those around you are on. One way to stay in touch is to pay attention to what people are saying and doing. It's also extremely important to pay attention to what *you* are saying and doing in relation to the change. Ask others how they see you reacting—knowing this will help you determine what actions you need to take as a change leader.

Finding out what people are saying and doing requires you to scan for information. First, you need to determine what information to seek. Generally, any information you gather should focus on three points:

- What's going well with the change?

- What needs to be done differently?

- How are people reacting?

Second, you need to determine your data collection method:

- *Observation.* Observation can give you an impression of the work, the people, and the climate of the organizational setting. Even a relatively unstructured approach such as observing what happens in a meeting can provide initial descriptive information.

- *Interviews.* Interviews can be conducted one-on-one or with small groups. The interviewer should not be someone who has a stake in the outcome of the data being gathered.

- *Survey.* A survey requires written responses to written questions. Typically, surveys are distributed to a group of people.

Each method has both pros and cons, as presented in the accompanying chart.

Comparison of Data Collection Methods

Method	Pros	Cons
Observation	• Allows you to draw conclusions based on what you see and hear rather than what you're told • Can be the most authentic way to gather data	• Time-consuming • Behavior may change as a result of being observed • Respondents may have concerns about how information will be used
Interviews	• Opportunity to ask for clarification of both questions and answers • Content can be unrestricted • Allows for in-depth conversation • Rich data—people like to talk	• Time-consuming • The way questions are asked can influence responses • Can be very subjective • Respondents may have concerns about how information will be used
Survey	• Easy to score or tabulate • Cheaper than interviews or observation • Responses can be anonymous • Less time spent personally data gathering • Can usually ask more questions	• No opportunity to probe the responses • No face-to-face contact • Time-consuming to develop • Respondents may have concerns about how information will be used • Negative reactions to completing forms • Questions can be misinterpreted

If you are considering using interviews or surveys, confer with someone who has experience in using those methods (Chapter 7 lists some references for these data-gathering techniques). As for observation, you can begin to do that now. Remember to ask others to make comments on what you are saying and doing.

Look back at your answers to questions 5 and 6 in Exercise 5. Do your responses give you any clues to your present level of reaction to change (denial, resistance, or commitment)? How about others? Following are some indicators of the three stages as well as some strategies for moving forward from the *denial* and *resistance* levels and then maintaining the *commitment* level:

Denial Stage

What you may be hearing:

- "This is a stupid idea."

- "This is the latest flavor of the month."

- "Someday they'll realize the disastrous results and admit their mistakes."

- "Remember how it used to be in the good old days?"

- "I've been here twenty-five years and nothing has changed."

- "Computers? My typewriter works just fine."

What you may be seeing:

- People continuing to perform as if nothing has happened
- People withdrawing from conversations about the change

What to do:

- Talk, talk, talk about the change.
- Share all the information you have, even if it is sketchy.
- Hold "town hall" meetings.
- Set up a hot line for information.
- Have people answer the questions posed in Exercise 3, "Are You Prepared?"

Resistance Stage

What you may be hearing:

- "I really will miss working with Ron and Larry."
- "Now I'll have to train someone who makes more money than I do."
- "Now I have to get approval before I make that purchase."
- "If I have to use the computer, fine. But isn't this clerical work?"

What you may be seeing:

- Increased use of sick hours

- Increased open questioning of authority

- Lower productivity

- Silence in meetings

What to do:

- Listen, listen, listen.

- Acknowledge feelings.

- Acknowledge losses.

- Develop clear roles, goals, and responsibilities.

- Lend support.

- React nondefensively.

- Obtain necessary training.

- Explore alternatives.

- Conduct brainstorming sessions.

- Take action on suggestions.

- Work with the resistance—solicit and listen to objections.

Commitment Level

What you may be hearing:

- "What is the best approach to this problem?"

- "Let's go out to lunch to celebrate."

- "I just learned a new software program. I have time at lunch if anyone wants to see how it works."

What you may be seeing:

- People engaged in vigorous discussions about the work processes(s)

- Positive customer survey results

- Use of problem-solving techniques

What to do:

- Reward people for doing the right things.

- Develop long-range goals.

- Celebrate successes.

- Hold sessions to continually track progress.

- Keep up-to-date on current trends in your industry or business.

- Continue to learn and provide learning opportunities for others.

- Share what you have learned.

Exercise 5 gave you the opportunity to assess how the change you're facing is going as well as to gauge reactions to the change. It's important to validate these steps with the people who will be affected by the change. A method of doing that comes in Chapter 4, which presents the third step of the Challenging Change model: exploring options for change.

Chapter Four

Explore Options for Change

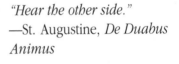

"Hear the other side."
—St. Augustine, *De Duabus Animus*

The third step in the Challenging Change model involves exploring options for change. To do that, you must share what you've discovered with the people you have observed, interviewed, and surveyed.

Both Judith and Tom have observed how others around them are reacting to change. In Judith's case, she has seen signs of worry in her employees and has heard comments from them about management's failure to communicate. She also knows she has been avoiding talking about the changes going on. Tom sees that his family has adjusted well to the change that brought them to their new home, and he knows he's presently feeling "paralyzed" about his options.

Until they share this data, their options are limited. Sharing what they've observed could open up lines of communication for Judith that currently don't exist, and Tom may find that his family members have some options for him that he can't see now because he feels so anxious.

Both Judith and Tom are acting as Lone Rangers. But the days of being the only one to look at and solve a problem rarely exist anymore.

Sharing the Data

Sharing your data in a way that produces results is tricky business—you want this to be a positive experience for both you and the others affected by the change. A trio of methods exists for sharing data:

1. *Compiling all the data and distributing copies to all parties affected by the data.* You may not want feedback; this option allows you to just share information.

2. *Reviewing the data, making a decision, and letting people know what the decision is.* The number of people involved in the decision making can range from just yourself to all affected by the change.

3. *Conducting a feedback meeting.* Here you present a picture of the current situation about the change face-to-face with the people it affects. You share data this way in order to validate it as well as to explore options regarding what to do with it.

As a change leader, never enter into a feedback meeting lightly—planning is necessary. Depending on the amount of data and the complexity of change(s) you are addressing, you may find it necessary to hold more than one meeting. If so, it's best to convene any subsequent meeting(s) soon, while the data is fresh. If at all possible, the meeting(s) should take place off-site, so ordinary distractions don't interfere.

In addition, seriously consider using a facilitator at feedback meetings. Although it's important for you to be an active participant, you should avoid influencing others to such a degree that they don't voice their real opinions. You may not intend to do that, but your position as change leader may have that result anyway. A facilitator can deal with this more easily than those directly involved.

Planning for the meeting and using the other tools and techniques discussed in this chapter will result in an effective feedback meeting. One mark of such a meeting is shared trust and focused dialogue. Exercise 6 poses some questions that will set the stage for that.

Exercise 6

What's Important to Know?

A tool that will strengthen your chances for an effective meeting is an agenda. Your answers to the questions in Exercise 6 are important to constructing one.

1. What is my objective in sharing the data I have collected with the other people in the meeting?

_____

_____

_____

_____

_____

_____

_____

_____

_____

_____

_____

2. What role do I see for myself at this meeting? Are there skills highlighted in Exercise 4 that will assist me in this role?

_____

_____

_____

_____

_____

_____

_____

_____

3. What do I want the people who will be attending the meeting to do?

_____

_____

_____

_____

_____

_____

_____

_____

Why an Agenda?

The message that's been building loud and clear in this book is threefold with regard to change:

1. It's important for you to know where you are going.

2. It's important for others to know where you are going.

3. It's important for others to know where they are going.

A well-prepared agenda serves as a road map for this process during the feedback meeting. Following are your basic components for the agenda at a feedback meeting:

- Purpose of the session

- Outcome

- Role clarification

- Ground rules

- Analysis of data

- Decision-making process

- Action-planning process

Purpose of the session. Have you ever attended a meeting and had no idea why you were there? Do you remember how you reacted? In Exercise 6, you answered the question "What is my objective in sharing the data I have collected with the other people in the meeting?" The reason for this question was to emphasize the importance of informing people why they are attending the meeting. That's why it's the first thing on the agenda. So tell them—right up front.

Outcome. Once you've told the participants why you've called them together, tell them what you hope to accomplish. For example, your desired outcome may be an action plan that addresses three things: that the change is implemented in a manner that builds on what's already going well with the change, which areas need to be dealt with differently, and how to move people to the commitment level.

Role clarification. Once you have clarified the purpose and outcome, you need to clarify what you will do and what you want others to do. Do you know what part you are to play at the meeting? Are you supposed to participate? Are you supposed to act as a sounding board? Are you supposed to lead the meeting? Are you supposed to participate in decision making? Do you know the parts others are supposed to play? The participants at your meeting will be asking the same questions and others. Your answers to questions 2 and 3 in Exercise 6 should provide guidance about this agenda item.

Ground rules. During any meeting, but especially one in which people are analyzing their own information, ground rules can keep the meeting on track and provide participants with a reference for measuring their performance. It's important that such rules be developed by the meeting participants and posted where all can see and refer to them. During long meetings, periodically reviewing the ground rules can keep the proceedings focused.

Here's a sample list of basic ground rules that your group can modify as appropriate:

- Be specific when discussing issues.

- Focus on action items to implement the change.

- Listen to others.

- Don't interrupt.

- Participate!

- Make decisions by _____. (After presenting the data to the participants, discuss how decisions will be made and add it to the ground rules.)

- Periodically review the ground rules to determine their usefulness.

Analysis of data. Here you have the opportunity to determine the validity of the data you have collected and begin analyzing it. There are four steps to this process:

1. Provide all affected participants with the results of your data collection.

2. Arrange the data in a manner that can easily be reviewed and discussed and also retains the respondents' anonymity.

3. Give the participants time to study the data and either confirm or refute it.

4. Discuss what the data provides, what's important, and why.

When data is analyzed, issues and solutions begin to emerge. To ensure the success of this portion of the feedback meeting, your communication competency and skills are extremely important. (Remember the question in Chapter 1, "Can you listen in a nonjudgmental way?") Listening is more than hearing—it's an active process, and one of the hardest things you will have to do as you explore options for change. You will have to both concentrate on and connect to what people are saying—really hear their words, really understand what they're telling you.

Many of the issues explored in the feedback meeting relate to how people are dealing with change, which probably will include some resistance to the change. As you review the data, the following suggestions can help you deal with resistance:

Do:

- Arrange the data to retain anonymity.

- Use nonjudgmental listening.

- Be specific in what you say.

- Focus on actions that are within your control.

- Take into account the needs of all involved.

- Check for understanding.

- Use the ground rules when necessary.

Don't:

- Become the answer person.

- Lecture.

- Judge what others are saying.

- Discount what others are saying.

Decision-making process. It's important that all participants understand the decision-making process to be used during the meeting. Although there are several ways to make decisions, consensus proves most effective during a feedback meeting when part of the purpose and outcome is to do some problem solving.

Before you accept this approach, it's important to understand exactly what consensus means. Consensus is "universal agreement." All the parties involved actively discuss issues surrounding any decisions, everyone pools their knowledge and experience, and any final decision must be supported by each participant. The decision must be one every participant can live with.

Consensus decision making requires more time than a majority vote because every participant has to either agree or at least be able to live with and support the decision. However, during change this is time well spent—involvement in decision making dramatically reduces resistance. Further, research indicates that the consensus approach to decision making results in a significantly higher quality decision than other methods.

There will be times, though, when the consensus process just isn't working or there isn't enough time to consider everyone's opinion. On such occasions, the following decision-making options are available:

- Defer the decision to a later time.

- Make the decision based on a majority vote.

- As the leader, make the decision based on input from participants.

If you use a decision-making process other than consensus, be sure that participants understand that commitment from everyone may be sacrificed. Be cautious in making a decision to use another method.

When you decide on what method will be used, add it to the ground rules.

Action-planning process. The payoff from a feedback meeting is that it holds the promise of everyone doing something and taking ownership of the change. This should be the intended outcome of most feedback meetings. Ownership can be established through action planning. Action planning is the point at which you and the other meeting participants really take charge of change. Chapter 5 presents this fourth step of the Challenging Change model: taking charge of change.

Chapter Five

Take Charge of Change

> *"Take calculated risks. That is quite
> different than being rash."*
> —George Patton, in a letter to his
> son dated June 6, 1944

After validating or revising your
perception of what's going well,
what you need to do differently,
and the levels of reaction that both
you and others are experiencing,
it's important to push forward, to
tackle the difficult task of
determining *what can be done*. It's
time to make decisions about what
you and the others affected by the

change can really do to take charge of the change event and your reactions to it. Taking charge includes taking calculated risks; it means being decisive, proactive, and purposeful. An action plan can assist you with that.

The Action Plan

Chapter 3 suggested some specific actions you can take to assist yourself and others with reactions to change. Now that everyone's reactions have been validated in the feedback meeting, it's time to share those "What to Do" suggestions. These actions are only a starting point, however. Do the other people involved see value in them? Are any other actions appropriate to take? Through continued interaction with the other participants, you will identify the various actions needed to tackle both the reactions and the actual change event. These steps should become items on an action plan.

An action plan will give you a structure for taking charge of change. A constructive action plan advances the successful beginning of an undertaking, its most important phase. It gives form to the "who, what, when, where, why, and how" details that need to be addressed. The following exercise will get you started on the preliminary questions for an action plan.

Exercise

7

What's Needed for Success?

Answer the following questions as they relate to the data that's been generated concerning the change. The questions should be completed by all involved at the feedback meeting.

1. What are the three most pressing issues concerning the change?

_____

_____

_____

_____

_____

2. Do you and the other participants have any control over these issues? If not, who do you need to contact or get involved with to help you with this change?

_____

_____

_____

_____

_____

3. How are the other participants reacting to the change? At which of the three levels (denial, resistance, commitment) are they operating on?

_____

_____

_____

_____

_____

4. What will success look like if the three issues listed in question 1 are resolved?

_____

_____

_____

_____

_____

5. Is it necessary for everyone to be at the commitment level for the success described in question 4 to occur?

_____

_____

_____

_____

_____

Action Items

The next step involves collectively identifying the specific actions, called action items, that will achieve the desired outcome. One way to do this is brainstorming, one of the most effective methods of rapidly listing ideas from all participants. After generating the ideas, the group should evaluate whether to include them in the action plan. A facilitator can be of great use here. For each action item selected, complete Exercise 8.

Exercise 8

Action Plan Items

For each action item you include in your action plan, answer the following questions.

1. Who can help you with this action?

_____

_____

_____

2. Is there anyone who can say "no" or raise any type of objection? Who is it?

_____

_____

_____

3. What can you do to obtain that person's support?

_____

_____

_____

4. What other obstacles, if any, stand in the way?

_____

_____

_____

5. What steps can be taken to alleviate the obstacles?

_____

_____

_____

6. What specific tasks will move you toward achieving the action?

_____

_____

_____

7. Who should be primarily responsible for this item?

_____

_____

_____

8. What is the target date for completion?

_____

_____

_____

The finished plan should be a written document listing—at a minimum—the action item, the primary responsible party, and the estimated completion date. Everyone should receive a copy.

Does this process seem overwhelming? If so, it may be because these are issues you've never considered before in addressing change. But if you have important issues (as stated in Exercise 7, question 1) that are unresolved, or people (including yourself) at the denial or resistance level of reaction, can you chance not addressing them? Spending time on these in the beginning can save a great deal of time later on.

So, Are You Done?

Not quite—every change must be monitored (you'll find out how in Chapter 6). And if your situation involves change at an organization you're associated with, keep this in mind:

All organizations are made up of several components, and the change you have identified relates to at least one of them:

- **Structure**—how the work of the organization is organized (by function, product, or a combination of both)

- **Tasks**—the work of the organization (the purpose for its existence)

- **People**—the individuals performing the tasks

- **Technology**—the tools, equipment, and procedures necessary to complete the work

To ensure success, you must now determine how the change you've identified may impact on the other components. The following exercise will assist you in this assessment.

Exercise 9

The Impact on Other Components

Answer the following questions as they relate to your specific change.

Structure

1. Is the work in your organization arranged by function, by product, or by some other method?

_____

_____

_____

_____

_____

2. If this structure impedes the change, how can the work be restructured?

_____

_____

_____

_____

_____

3. Do your responses to questions 1 and 2 identify additional action items needed to support the change? If so, note them here and add them to your plan.

_____

_____

_____

_____

_____

Tasks

1. What tasks are currently performed in your work group?

_____

_____

_____

_____

_____

2. How does the change impact these tasks?

_____

_____

_____

_____

_____

3. Does your work group need to focus on different tasks because of the change?

_____

_____

_____

_____

_____

4. Are the right people assembled to complete the tasks identified in question 3? If not, what changes need to be made?

_____

_____

_____

_____

_____

5. Do your responses to questions 1 to 4 identify additional actions needed to support the change? If so, note them here and add them to the action plan.

_____

_____

_____

_____

People

1. Are different skills needed as a result of the change?

_____

_____

_____

_____

_____

2. Does the current reward system reflect the tasks needed due to the change? What tasks result in rewards? Are these the same tasks that meet the needs of your customers?

_____

_____

_____

_____

3. If teamwork is required as a result of the change, what team skills have been developed and are people rewarded for using them and reaching team goals?

_____

_____

_____

_____

4. Do your responses to questions 1 to 3 identify additional action items needed to support the change? If so, note them here and add them to the action plan.

_____

_____

_____

_____

_____

Technology

1. What technology are you using? Is it adequate to meet the needs of the change?

_____

_____

_____

_____

_____

2. Are your communication systems adequate to meet the needs of the change?

_____

_____

_____

_____

3. Do you have the proper software and hardware in place to accomplish the tasks required by the change?

_____

_____

_____

_____

_____

4. Do your responses to questions 1 to 3 identify additional action items needed to support the change? If so, note them here and add them to the action plan.

_____

_____

_____

_____

_____

With the help of others, you have developed an action plan that addresses not only action steps relating to the change but also the reactions others are having toward it. This plan enables you to take charge of change—which means not only developing but also implementing your actions. Now it is critical for everyone involved to become accountable for the action items. It is time to look at the final step of the Challenging Change model: monitoring change.

Chapter Six

Monitor Change

"*Possible? Is anything impossible?*
Read the newspaper."
—Duke of Wellington

Participating in a feedback
meeting, reviewing and analyzing
data, and agreeing to action items
can be exciting. This process
presents an opportunity to focus
on important matters without
interruption. At the end of a
productive meeting, participants
feel truly committed to the plan.
However, upon leaving the cocoon
of the meeting room, telephones

start to ring, customer requests and complaints roll in, rumors begin, deadlines slip...

Given the daily actions and decisions that produce even more changes, how can you ensure that what you accomplished in the first four steps of the Challenging Change model occurs? One way is to monitor change.

Three operations work together to effectively monitor change:

- Measuring

- Learning

- Celebrating

All three should be included in the action plan.

Measuring Success

Measurement is crucial to your success in monitoring change. It is imperative to have a method in place for measuring whether you've attained your action plan items. You began to consider this when you answered question 4 in Exercise 7, which asked what success would look like.

You need to be precise. If you answered that success would be "satisfied customers," what does that really mean? Can you measure satisfaction? Not really. What you *can* measure are fewer complaints along with increased orders. If you answered that success would be "improved morale," how will you measure that? Perhaps through decreased absenteeism, increased productivity, increased employee suggestions, and so on.

Keep two important points in mind in determining your measurement of what success looks like:

1. Involve those affected by the change in deciding what should be measured to determine success. They know what is important to them.

2. Consider how the measurement you establish could affect the other components involved. For instance, if one measure of success you choose is to decrease the time spent with customers on the phone, do you have mechanisms to ensure that the quality of the customer contact remains acceptable?

Go back to your answers in Exercise 7 and evaluate whether the success you have chosen lends itself to a method of measurement. If not, rework your vision so that it does. The following exercise should assist you in this task.

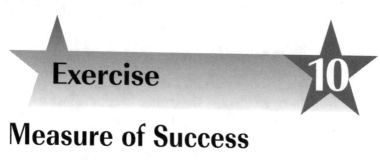

Measure of Success

1. How specifically will you know when you have attained success? Are your measures attainable?

_____

_____

_____

_____

2. Do your measures complement each other? Have you looked at potential conflicts?

_____

_____

_____

_____

3. How did you involve customers and others who will be carrying out the action steps in the development of the measures?

_____

_____

_____

4. How will you explain these measures to customers and those doing the work?

_____

_____

_____

_____

_____

_____

5. Are these measures cost effective? Are they worth the time and effort necessary to monitor them?

_____

_____

_____

_____

_____

_____

An effective measurement strategy will be consistent with organizational goals, easy to track, and attainable. Regarding the tracking aspect, use data collection methods such as those discussed in Chapter 3 to gather the information necessary to monitor your progress.

Learning From Change

The second requisite for effectively monitoring change is to learn from it. Why reinvent the wheel each time a change comes along? Certain behaviors should become second nature. It would be useful for you and others involved in the change you are facing to answer the questions posed in Exercise 11, perhaps four to six weeks after you've written the action plan. No matter how you gather the information (meeting as a group to answer the questions or asking people to fill out the questionnaire individually), remember to share the results just as you have the other data you've gathered.

Exercise 11

What Have You Learned?

1. What have you learned about your own attitudes or assumptions about change as a result of being involved in planning for the change you have identified?

_____

_____

_____

_____

2. What behavioral change, if any, did you personally try out?

_____

_____

_____

_____

3. What do you think the others involved in the change have learned at this stage of implementation?

_____

_____

_____

_____

4. What has worked well so far?

_____

_____

_____

_____

5. What do you think needs to be done differently?

_____

_____

_____

_____

6. Describe at least one challenge or problem you are willing to discuss with others involved in this change.

_____

_____

_____

_____

7. What is one tool, technique, or strategy that has worked for you in working through this change?

_____

_____

_____

Once you gather the data, explore with the others what needs to be done. You may need to refine some of the action items. You may need to refine the measurement system itself. Or you may need to use failure as a learning opportunity. You definitely need to celebrate any success you have attained. Celebration is the third requisite for monitoring change.

Celebrating

It's extremely important to celebrate your progress, and it's also easy to not make time for it. When and how should you celebrate? Celebrations should be meaningful to those who are being acknowledged and praised. The following exercise can help you plan these celebrations.

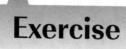

Exercise

Pat Yourselves on the Back!

With the assistance of those affected by the change, complete the following questions.

1. When and how do we usually recognize accomplishments?

_____

_____

_____

_____

_____

_____

2. Is this method acceptable for celebrating our progress with this change?

_____

_____

_____

_____

_____

_____

3. What should we celebrate?

_____

_____

_____

_____

_____

_____

_____

4. How and when should we celebrate?

_____

_____

_____

_____

_____

_____

_____

_____

_____

With continuous change, it's hard enough to take time to step back and take the time to plan for it. Celebration often is one of the lowest priorities (and frequently not a priority at all). It's up to you to consciously provide the acknowledgment of "Hey—we did it, and we did it together." Because around the corner is the new technology, the new product line, the new customer, and the new boss. The better people feel about what they have accomplished, the better they can face these new challenges.

As change is continuous, you're never really finished. Challenging change ultimately relates to how well you and others become continuous learners in a regularly changing environment. Challenging change offers you the opportunity to experiment, and it reinforces teamwork. Challenging change enhances both individual and collective competencies, resulting in continuous learning. Challenging change at both the individual and organizational levels requires moving ahead—not simply chugging along in place. The final chapter will summarize the key points to help you *challenge* change.

Chapter Seven

Challenge Change

"A good beginning makes a good ending." —English proverb

As stated from the outset, the ultimate goal of the five-step Challenging Change model is to help you steer successfully through change rather than ignore it or feel overwhelmed by it. Review the steps each time you face change, and share them with others who are also affected. This process can become second nature, part of your natural way of approaching change.

As you work on making this model a practical, even intuitive response to change, here are the highlights and the key points to keep in sight.

- *Be proactive.* Constant change has become the status quo. Rather than just reacting, keep alert to what is going on around you.

- *Be aware of how you live your life in a constantly changing world.* Pick a day and pay attention to how you react to all that is required of you. What are your immediate responses? Your immediate gut feelings? Your immediate frustrations? Your immediate approvals? Do they match up with how you wish you had responded?

- *Be aware of how others live their lives in a constantly changing world.* Pick one day for observing how someone else reacts to daily demands. Is there something you can learn from that person? Ask yourself this from two views—what do you admire about how he or she has reacted, and what do you hope you don't do that he or she has done?

- *Consider both the change event and the reactions to the change.* If you or others are at the denial level or resistance level of reaction for a long enough period, you may have a natural tendency to assume the change is the problem. That may be true at times, but don't overlook that sometimes it's your reaction to the change that creates the obstacles.

- *Don't look to the Lone Ranger to be your role model.* Rarely does it make sense to act on your own without input from others. (This is also a good time to remind you to use a facilitator at your feedback meetings.)

- *Don't give up.* You and others will be practicing some new behaviors, so don't expect perfection or a complete sense of comfort at first. In the wonderful children's book by Shel Silverstein, *The Missing Piece Meets the Big O,* the author illustrates what happens when new behaviors are practiced. At first things are bumpy, but after a short while it's smooth going. Buy this book for a child, but keep it for yourself.

- *Know what success looks like.* Be sure you have a measurement system and that it is measuring the right things.

- *Take time to celebrate.* Reward yourself and others throughout the change process.

- *Prepare for change, face the change, explore options for change, take charge of change, and monitor change.* In other words, challenge change.

Exercise 1 asked you to answer some questions intended to start you thinking about your approach to change. You were instructed to answer them quickly and with little thought. Since completing that exercise, you've put thought and action into your approach to change. This last exercise asks you to revisit these questions because your daily life is affected by most of them.

Exercise 13

Revisiting What's Happening to You

Three changes have been made to this exercise since you reacted to these questions in Chapter 1. The questions are divided around the competencies presented in Chapter 3, extra comments have been added to some of the questions (in **bold** print), and this time you should take some time to prepare your answers.

Communication

1. How do you articulate your goals and expectations?

_____

_____

_____

2. Do you know how to give constructive feedback? Do you know how to receive it? **Give recent examples of both.**

_____

_____

_____

3. Can you listen in a nonjudgmental way? **What have you been told about the way you listen?**

_____

_____

_____

Problem Solving

1. What techniques have you developed for dealing with change? **Refer to Chapter 1, Exercise 2, Question 2.**

_____

_____

_____

2. What techniques for dealing with change do you see in others you work with? Or live with?

_____

_____

_____

3. What two things went really well for you recently? What was your role in each? **Refer to Chapter 1, Exercise 2, Question 1.**

_____

_____

_____

4. What two things didn't go so well? What was your role?

_____

_____

_____

5. When several things are going on at the same time, how do you decide which changes to pay attention to? **Refer to Chapter 3, Exercise 5, Question 1.**

_____

_____

_____

Motivation

1. How do you keep motivated?

_____

_____

_____

2. If you have young children, do you yell at them to "stop yelling"? **If you do, are you motivating them to do what you ask (or in this case, yell)? Albert Schweitzer once said, "Example is not the main thing in influencing others, it's the only thing." In other words, do you walk your talk as a change leader?**

_____

_____

_____

3. How do you reward yourself?

_____

_____

_____

4. How do you acknowledge the contributions of others? At work? At home?

_____

_____

_____

5. What do you do to relax? Do you relax?

_____

_____

_____

6. In times of change, do you consider what has stayed stable in your life and how that can help?

_____

_____

_____

7. What kind of person were you when you chose your current career? Have you changed? What prompted those changes?

_____

_____

_____

8. If you are a manager, what managerial skills do you have?

_____

_____

_____

9. If you have employees, how do you think they view you? Do they look to you for direction? Do you want them to?

_____

_____

_____

10. If you have children, how do you think they view you? Do they look to you for direction? Do you want them to?

_____

_____

_____

11. How many career changes have you made?

_____

_____

_____

12. How many times have you moved?

_____

_____

_____

13. How many changes have you had in significant relationships? **Do you ever stop to think of the reactions you may be having to these changes (in questions 11, 12, and 13) and the effect (positive or negative) this may exert on how you keep motivated during changes like these?**

_____

_____

_____

Innovation

1. What recent risk have you taken and what did you learn from this experience?

_____

_____

_____

2. Can you play Nintendo? Do you know what Nintendo is?

_____

_____

_____

3. If you have teenagers, have you ever said, "You call that music?" If so, do you know what music you were talking about? **Bottom line here—do you keep up to date on social or generational changes?**

_____

_____

_____

4. Are you willing to try new ideas and approaches to issues? **Name two. Also, check how you scored yourself in Chapter 2, Exercise 3, Question 1.**

_____

_____

_____

5. What do you believe are some of the old ways of doing business that cannot lead businesses into the future?

_____

_____

_____

6. How do you scan for information you need?

_____

_____

_____

Focus on Customers

1. How do you measure customer needs? Customer satisfaction?

_____

_____

_____

2. If you own a business, what is your vision for it? How do you know if you're headed for it?

_____

_____

_____

3. How do you keep up to date on government policies or regulations that may affect your business?

_____

_____

_____

Continuous Learning

1. Do you use the latest technology to its fullest potential for your needs in your business life? In your personal life? **How do you do this?**

_____

_____

_____

2. Do you ever say, "I never would have thought of that"? **Under what circumstances?**

_____

_____

_____

3. What new skill(s) have you learned this year? What have you taught someone else this year?

_____

_____

_____

4. Do you ever talk to others about how they handle change? **If so, what have you learned? Also, how did you score yourself in Chapter 2, Exercise 3, Question 2?**

_____

_____

_____

5. What are your hot buttons? What or who has pushed them lately? **How do you get over it?**

_____

_____

_____

6. Can you admit when you just don't know? **When was the last time you did that? How did you score yourself in Chapter 2, Exercise 3, Question 3?**

_____

_____

_____

7. Two years ago, you never would have thought you would do what?

_____

_____

_____

As stressed throughout this book, change is constant in today's environment. Winston Churchill once said, "To improve is to change; to be perfect is to change often." Your ability to challenge change gives you the opportunity to live his words.

Postscript

It's one year since Judith was sitting in her car waiting for the light to change and reflecting on all that had happened at work. Today she's sitting in a traffic jam that doesn't appear as if it's going to clear up for quite some time. She laughs because she just recalled a conversation she had with an acquaintance, Ellen, earlier that day. The woman had found out that Judith's daughter Molly had married six months earlier. When she learned that Molly had married Randy, Ellen said, "Oh, is he the one you always called weird Randy?" Judith replied: "I used to. But now I find him quite interesting. He recently talked me into learning to kayak. I still disagree with him at times, but we have more in common than I would have ever thought. I started listening to him more than I used to."

She also reflects on what has become an ongoing and fruitful dialogue with her employees. The accomplishment she is proudest of was their decision, as a group, to raise some of their concerns with her boss about the reorganization. In addition to increased communication about options available within the company, her boss contracted with a number of external consultants to assist in the areas of customer service, team building, and outplacement options for the employees whose jobs were abolished. Tomorrow her boss is holding the first "town hall" meeting with employees and some key customers to discuss the progress that has been made.

Tom was one who took advantage of the outplacement opportunities offered. This was after he had started to explore options with his family. As a family, they concluded they would like to stay where they were. His two teenagers agreed to go to state colleges to hold down tuition costs if that would help them stay in their new home. It did. After carefully examining their finances, Tom realized he could take a cut in salary. He is currently working part-time as a consultant to businesses on personnel issues. He is also teaching twice a week at a local college, and his travel time is now strictly *personal*.

Bibliography & Suggested Reading

Bennis, Warren, and Burt Nanus. *Leaders: The Strategies for Taking Charge.* New York: Harper & Row, 1985.

Bradburn, N., and S. Sudman & Associates. *Improving Interview Methods and Questionnaire Design.* San Francisco, CA: Jossey-Bass, 1979.

Bridges, William. *Managing Transitions: Making the Most of Change.* Reading, MA: Addison-Wesley, 1991.

Bridges, William. *Transitions: Making Sense of Life's Changes.* Reading, MA: Addison-Wesley, 1980.

Fink, A., and J. Kosecoff. *How to Conduct Surveys.* Beverly Hills, CA: Sage Publications, 1985.

Lowenthal, Jeffrey N. *Reengineering the Organization: A Step-by-Step Approach to Corporate Revitalization.* Milwaukee, WI: ASQC Quality Press, 1994.

Noer, David M. *Healing the Wounds: Overcoming the Trauma of Layoffs and Revitalizing Downsized Organizations*. San Francisco, CA: Jossey-Bass, 1993.

Peters, Tom. *Thriving on Chaos: A Handbook for a Management Revolution*. New York: Alfred A. Knopf, 1987.

Pritchett, Price, and Ron Pound. *A Survival Guide to the Stress of Organizational Change*. Dallas, TX: Pritchett & Associates, 1995.

Silverstein, Shel. *The Missing Piece Meets the Big O*. New York: Harper & Row, 1981.

Spencer, Sabina, and John D. Adams. *Life Changes: Growing Through Personal Transitions*. San Luis Obispo, CA: Impact Publishers, 1990.

Weisbord, Marvin R. *Discovering Common Ground*. San Francisco, CA: Berrett-Koehler, 1992.

Available From SkillPath Publications

Self-Study Sourcebooks

Climbing the Corporate Ladder: What You Need to Know and Do to Be a Promotable Person *by Barbara Pachter and Marjorie Brody*

Coping With Supervisory Nightmares: 12 Common Nightmares of Leadership and What You Can Do About Them *by Michael and Deborah Singer Dobson*

Discovering Your Purpose *by Ivy Haley*

Going for the Gold: Winning the Gold Medal for Financial Independence *by Lesley D. Bissett, CFP*

The Innovative Secretary *by Marlene Caroselli, Ed.D.*

Mastering the Art of Communication: Your Keys to Developing a More Effective Personal Style *by Michelle Fairfield Poley*

Organized for Success! 95 Tips for Taking Control of Your Time, Your Space, and Your Life *by Nanci McGraw*

P.E.R.S.U.A.D.E.: Communication Strategies That Move People to Action *by Marlene Caroselli, Ed.D.*

Productivity Power: 250 Great Ideas for Being More Productive *by Jim Temme*

Promoting Yourself: 50 Ways to Increase Your Prestige, Power, and Paycheck *by Marlene Caroselli, Ed.D.*

Proof Positive: How to Find Errors Before They Embarrass *by Karen L. Anderson*

Risk-Taking: 50 Ways to Turn Risks Into Rewards *by Marlene Caroselli, Ed.D. and David Harris*

Stress Control: How You Can Find Relief From Life's Daily Stress *by Steve Bell*

The Business and Technical Writer's Guide *by Robert McGraw*

Total Quality Customer Service: How to Make It Your Way of Life *by Jim Temme*

Write It Right! A Guide for Clear and Correct Writing *by Richard Andersen and Helene Hinis*

Handbooks

The ABC's of Empowered Teams: Building Blocks for Success *by Mark Towers*

Assert Yourself! Developing Power-Packed Communication Skills to Make Your Points Clearly, Confidently, and Persuasively *by Lisa Contini*

Breaking the Ice: How to Improve Your On-the-Spot Communication Skills *by Deborah Shouse*

The Care and Keeping of Customers: A Treasury of Facts, Tips, and Proven Techniques for Keeping Your Customers Coming BACK! *by Roy Lantz*

Challenging Change: Five Steps for Dealing With Change *by Holly DeForest and Mary Steinberg*

Dynamic Delegation: A Manager's Guide for Active Empowerment *by Mark Towers*

Every Woman's Guide to Career Success *by Denise M. Dudley*

Great Openings and Closings: 28 Ways to Launch and Land Your Presentations With Punch, Power, and Pizazz *by Mari Pat Varga*

Hiring and Firing: What Every Manager Needs to Know *by Marlene Caroselli, Ed.D. with Laura Wyeth, Ms.Ed.*

How to Be a More Effective Group Communicator: Finding Your Role and Boosting Your Confidence in Group Situations *by Deborah Shouse*

How to Deal With Difficult People *by Paul Friedman*

Learning to Laugh at Work: The Power of Humor in the Workplace *by Robert McGraw*

Making Your Mark: How to Develop a Personal Marketing Plan for Becoming More Visible and More Appreciated at Work *by Deborah Shouse*

Meetings That Work *by Marlene Caroselli, Ed.D.*

The Mentoring Advantage: How to Help Your Career Soar to New Heights *by Pam Grout*

Minding Your Business Manners: Etiquette Tips for Presenting Yourself Professionally in Every Business Situation *by Marjorie Brody and Barbara Pachter*

Misspeller's Guide *by Joel and Ruth Schroeder*

Motivation in the Workplace: How to Motivate Workers to Peak Performance and Productivity *by Barbara Fielder*

NameTags Plus: Games You Can Play When People Don't Know What to Say *by Deborah Shouse*

Networking: How to Creatively Tap Your People Resources *by Colleen Clarke*

New & Improved! 25 Ways to Be More Creative and More Effective *by Pam Grout*

The Power of Positivity: Eighty ways to energize your life *by Joel and Ruth Schroeder*

Power Write! A Practical Guide to Words That Work *by Helene Hinis*

Putting Anger to Work For You! *by Ruth and Joel Schroeder*

Reinventing Your Self: 28 Strategies for Coping With Change *by Mark Towers*

Saying "No" to Negativity: How to Manage Negativity in Yourself, Your Boss, and Your Co-Workers *by Zoie Kaye*

The Supervisor's Guide: The Everyday Guide to Coordinating People and Tasks *by Jerry Brown and Denise Dudley, Ph.D.*

Taking Charge: A Personal Guide to Managing Projects and Priorities *by Michal E. Feder*

Treasure Hunt: 10 Stepping Stones to a New and More Confident You! *by Pam Grout*

A Winning Attitude: How to Develop Your Most Important Asset! *by Michelle Fairfield Poley*

For more information, call 1-800-873-7545.